The Best Book of
Spaceships

Ian Graham

KINGFISHER
NEW YORK

Author: Ian Graham
Managing Editor: Camilla Hallinan
Series Editor: Sue Nicholson
Illustrators: Gary Bines,
  Lee Gibbons, Ceri Llewellyn
Art Editor: Ch'en-Ling
Art Director and cover design:
  Terry Woodley
Series Designer: Ben White
Production Controller: Kelly Johnson

Photographs on p. 26 by Martin
  Redfern/NASA

KINGFISHER
LONDON & NEW YORK

Distributed in the U.S. by Macmillan,
175 Fifth Ave., New York, NY 10010
Distributed in Canada by H.B. Fenn and Company Ltd.,
34 Nixon Road, Bolton, Ontario L7E 1W2

LIBRARY OF CONGRESS CATALOGING-IN-PUBLICATION DATA
Graham, Ian.
   The best book of spaceships / Ian Graham.—1st ed.
       p.   cm.
   Summary: Illustrations and text describe how humans
have tried to learn more about space and some of the
equipment and vehicles used to do this.
    1. Space vehicles—Juvenile literature. [I. Outer space—
Exploration. 2. Space vehicles.]   I. Title.
TL793.G688   1998
629.47—dc21   97-51599   CIP AC

ISBN 978-0-7534-6167-9

Kingfisher books are available for special promotions and
premiums. For details contact: Special Markets Department,
Macmillan, 175 Fifth Avenue, New York, NY 10010.

For more information, please visit www.kingfisherpublications.com

First published in 1998
First published in this format in 2007

Printed in Taiwan
10 9 8 7 6 5 4 3 2
2TR/0609/SAP/PICA(PICA)/126.6MA/F

Contents

Looking into space

For thousands of years, people have gazed in wonder at the night sky. Slowly, they learned more and more about the twinkling stars and the planets above them. Many dreamed of visiting and exploring the planets, but there was no way of traveling there. Instead, people had to make do with fuzzy views seen through telescopes.

Nowadays, we have all types of spacecraft that can travel into space, visit the planets, and even land on them.

Pathfinder explorer on Mars

Robot explorers

Robot explorers have become our eyes and ears on distant worlds we have not yet visited ourselves.

What's in space?

Earth is one of nine planets that fly through space around the Sun. The path that each planet follows as it flies around the Sun is called an orbit. Earth takes one year to orbit the Sun once. The Sun is enormous. One million Earths could fit inside it with lots of room to spare.

The pull of gravity

Gravity is an invisible force that pulls things toward it. The Sun is so big, its pull of gravity is strong enough to hold all the planets in their orbits.

Mercury
The closest planet to the Sun

The Sun
The star at the center of our solar system

Venus
A boiling-hot planet where it rains acid

Asteroids
Lumps of rock orbiting the Sun

Earth's moon

Earth
Our home planet

Stars
The Sun and stars that we can see from Earth are part of a huge group, or galaxy, called the Milky Way

Mars
A red and rocky planet

Jupiter
The biggest planet in the solar system

The solar system

The solar system is the name given to the Sun's family. It includes the planets and their moons, comets, and all the lumps of rock, dust, and ice that orbit the Sun.

Comet
A lump of icy rock that sprouts a bright tail as it nears the Sun

Pluto
The farthest planet from the Sun

Neptune
A beautiful blue planet streaked with white clouds

Saturn
A planet surrounded by beautiful rings

Uranus
A planet tipped over on its side

Far, far beyond our galaxy are other galaxies containing billions of stars

Rocket power

A rocket blasts off from its launch pad and soars into the sky with flames streaming from its engines.

As it climbs higher and higher, the air that is around it becomes thinner and thinner until there is none at all. The rocket has reached space.

Blast off!

When people wanted to launch machines into space, they had to invent rockets to carry them there. Only rockets are powerful enough to escape the pull of Earth's gravity.

Staging

A rocket is made up of
parts called stages. When
each stage has used up its
fuel, it is dropped to save
weight. The rest of the
rocket goes on into space.

Spacecraft

The top of the rocket then
opens, and a spacecraft
comes out. Some spacecraft
circle Earth. Others are
carried deeper into space
by more powerful rockets.

Apollo spacecraft

Saturn V
Height:
365 feet
Carried Apollo
spacecraft and
astronauts to
the Moon
between 1969
and 1972

All types of rockets

Every spacecraft and satellite sent
into space has been carried there
by a rocket. The first rockets were
relatively small and could only lift a
small weight. So the first spacecraft
and satellites had to be small, too.
As people learned more about how
to make rockets and how to launch
them, the rockets became bigger
and more powerful. Bigger rockets
can launch bigger spacecraft.

The biggest rocket ever built
was the American Saturn V Moon
rocket. (The "V" stands for "5.")

Ariane 4
Height:
175–190 feet
Since 1981,
Ariane rockets
have launched
many satellites
from French
Guiana
in South
America

Vostok spacecraft

Mercury spacecraft

Redstone
Height:
80 feet
Carried the
Mercury
spacecraft
and the first
American
astronauts
into space
in 1961

A-class
Height:
110 feet
Carried the
first Russian
satellite into
space in 1957,
also the first
living creature
(a dog named
Laika), in 1957
and in 1961,
the first human
being—Yuri
Gagarin

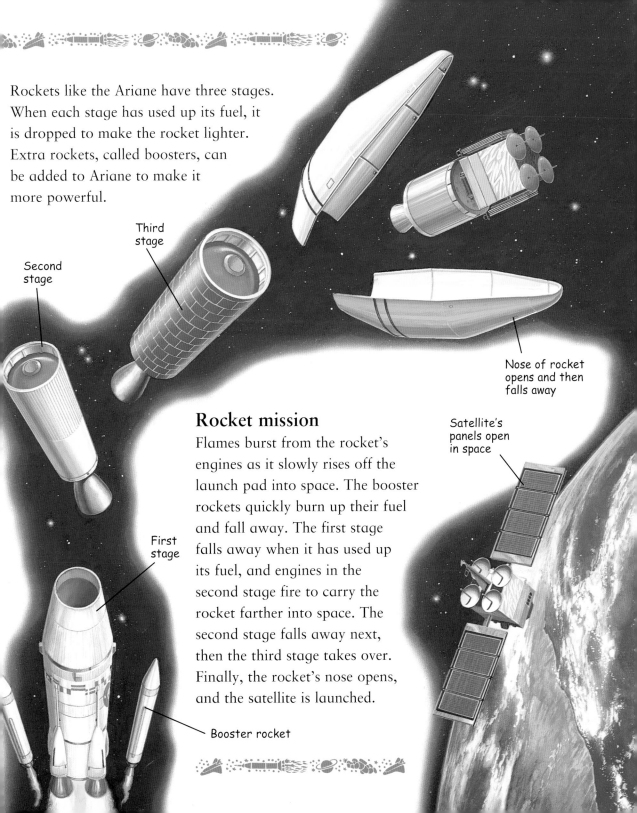

Rockets like the Ariane have three stages. When each stage has used up its fuel, it is dropped to make the rocket lighter. Extra rockets, called boosters, can be added to Ariane to make it more powerful.

Third stage

Second stage

Nose of rocket opens and then falls away

Satellite's panels open in space

Rocket mission

Flames burst from the rocket's engines as it slowly rises off the launch pad into space. The booster rockets quickly burn up their fuel and fall away. The first stage falls away when it has used up its fuel, and engines in the second stage fire to carry the rocket farther into space. The second stage falls away next, then the third stage takes over. Finally, the rocket's nose opens, and the satellite is launched.

First stage

Booster rocket

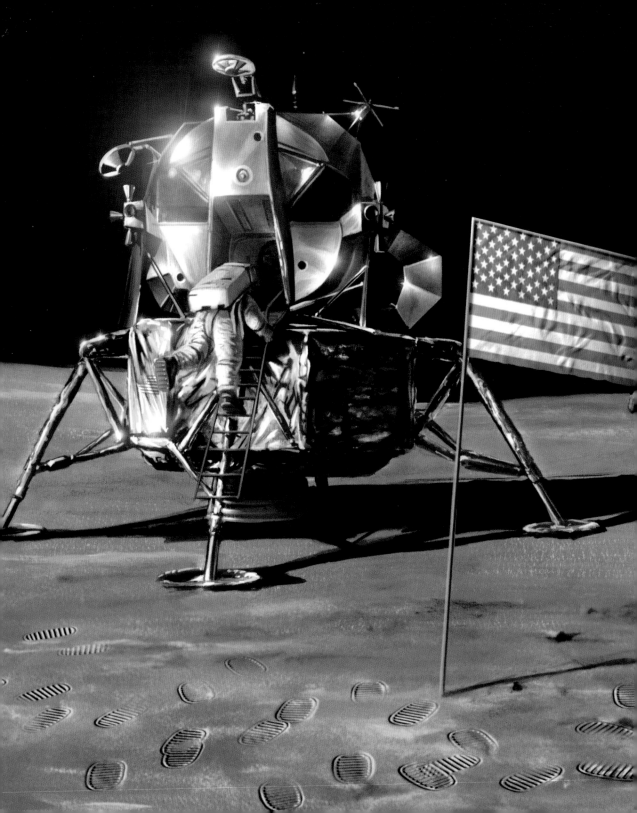

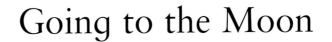

Going to the Moon

In July 1969, millions of people all over the world turned on their televisions at the same time. They were watching something that had never ever been seen before—an astronaut climbing out of a spacecraft that had just landed on the Moon. It was the first time that anyone from Earth had walked on another world.

◀ When the astronaut Neil Armstrong stepped onto the dusty surface of the Moon, he was farther away from home than any other explorer had ever been.

Moon Buggy

On later Moon missions, astronauts took a special car to the Moon called a Lunar Rover, or Moon Buggy. It helped them get around the Moon's rocky surface more easily.

Service Module
Carried supplies such as fuel and oxygen

Command Module
Apollo's control center and living quarters

Lunar Module
Landed on the Moon

The Moon is our closest neighbor in space, but it is still 239,000 miles away. Altogether, 27 astronauts have flown to the Moon, and 12 have landed on its dusty, rocky surface.

Apollo spacecraft

The Apollo spacecraft was made up of three parts, called modules. The Lunar Module was the only part of the spacecraft that landed on the Moon. The Command Module was the only part that came back to Earth. The spacecraft had to carry everything that the astronauts needed for their mission—including the air that they breathed.

Apollo Moon mission

◀ Flames shot from the five engines at the bottom of the huge Saturn V rocket. Then it slowly rose off the launch pad and climbed into the sky. The deafening roar from its engines made the ground shake.

▲ Three hours after takeoff, the Command and Service Modules separated from the Saturn V rocket. They turned around and joined with the Lunar Module.

3 The Apollo spacecraft then went on into space. It took three days for the astronauts to travel to the Moon.

4 Two astronauts floated down a tunnel into the Lunar Module and flew it to the Moon. The third stayed in the Command Module.

5 The astronauts explored the Moon's surface and collected rocks. They also raised the American flag. There is no breeze on the Moon, so the flag was held open by a stiff wire. The flag—and the astronauts' footprints—are still on the Moon.

Moon rocks

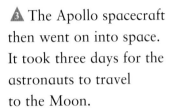

6 To leave the Moon, the Lunar Module split in two. Its top half blasted off, using the bottom as a launch pad.

7 The Lunar Module linked with the Command Module. It was then cut loose because it was not needed any more.

8 The Command Module separated from the Service Module. It glowed brightly in the sky as it entered the air around Earth. Parachutes opened to slow it down before it splashed into the sea. The crew was soon picked up by a waiting ship.

Shuttle power

Most rockets and spacecraft are used only once. This is an incredibly expensive way of sending machines and people into space—no one would build a jumbo jet and throw it away after only one flight! A rocket-powered spacecraft called a space shuttle is different because it can be used over and over again. It blasts off from a launch pad like a rocket, but then it lands on a runway like an airplane.

Space junk

Space junk is a serious problem for astronauts working in space. Parts of old rockets and broken satellites still orbit Earth. If they collide, the fuel inside them may explode, sending pieces of metal flying in all directions.

Astronauts weigh nothing
in space. When they leave
their spacecraft, they have
to clip themselves to it so
that they don't float away.
This astronaut is repairing
a broken satellite. His feet
are safely clipped to the space
shuttle's long robot arm.

The space shuttle

The shuttle is one of
the most complicated
machines ever built.
There is nothing else
like it. It can fly in the
air like an aircraft and
also move through
space like a rocket.

Booster
rocket

Satellite

Robot arm
helps move
satellites

Flight
deck

Orbiter

The main part of the
shuttle is a spacecraft
with wings, called the
orbiter. It is carried
into space by three
large rocket engines
and two booster
rockets.

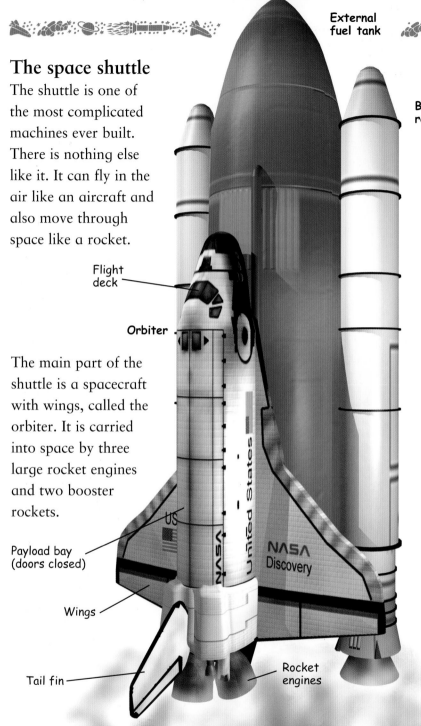

United States

NASA
Discovery

Payload bay
(doors open)

The space shuttle
carries satellites into
space in its payload
bay. Sometimes it brings
broken satellites back
to Earth for repair. On
some missions, it carries
a laboratory called the
Spacelab, in which
scientists do experiments
in space.

Payload bay
(doors closed)

Wings

Tail fin

Rocket
engines

In orbit

Doors open, and
satellite is launched

Doors
close

Fuel
tank
falls
away

Rockets
fire

Shuttle mission

The space shuttle soars into the
sky from its launch pad. The
booster rockets and the external
fuel tank fall away when they
have used up all their fuel.

In space, the astronauts
launch a satellite with the help
of the orbiter's long robot arm.

At the end of the mission, the
orbiter's rocket engines fire to
slow it down, and it begins to
fall back to Earth. It glows with
heat as it plunges back into the
air around Earth. Then it glides
down and lands on a runway
like a plane.

Reenters
Earth's
atmosphere

Booster
rockets
fall away

Shuttle
takes off

Boosters parachute
into the sea and are
used again

Glides back
to Earth

19

Space suits

In space there is no air. Anything that the Sun shines on is boiling hot, and anything in the shade is freezing cold. Human beings cannot live in space. We need air to breathe, and we need to be at the right temperature—not too hot and not too cold.

A spacecraft has to provide astronauts with air to breathe, and it has to keep them warm. When astronauts leave the spacecraft, they must wear a space suit, which performs the same task.

Gas thruster

Adjustable arm

Hand controller

Nitrogen gas tank

Gas thruster

Manned Maneuvering Unit (MMU) helps astronauts fly around outside the shuttle

Life-support backpack

TV camera

Putting on a space suit

This space suit is called the space shuttle EMU, which is short for Extravehicular Mobility Unit. The suit has a special backpack that keeps fresh air flowing through the suit.

Parts of a space suit

All the parts of a space suit lock together at the neck, waist, wrists, and ankles, so that the air inside cannot escape.

Gloves

Top

Control panel

Helmet

Legs

Radio headset

The long underwear is covered with thin plastic tubes that contain water. Heating or cooling the water keeps the astronaut at the right temperature.

Boots

Underwear

Life-support backpack

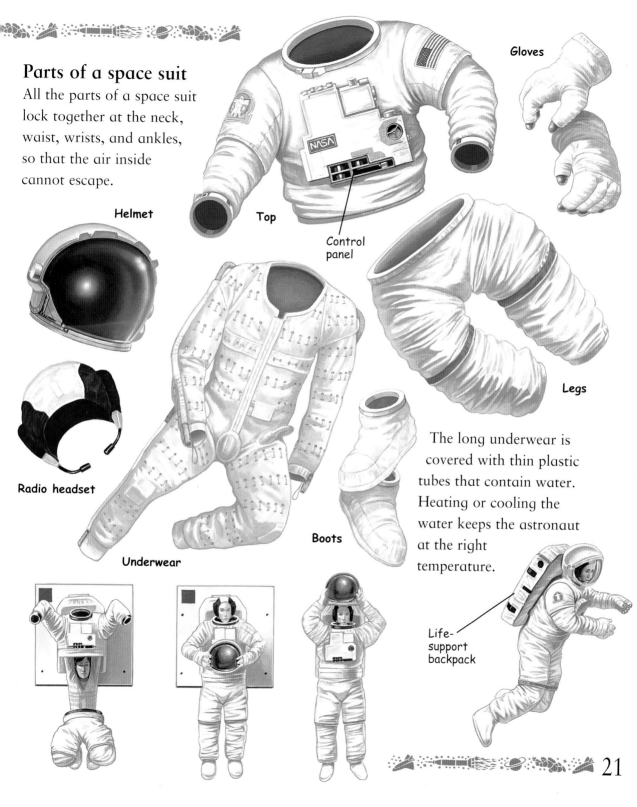

Working in space

Every day's work on board the space shuttle is set out in the flight plan for the mission. A typical mission may take ten days.

▶ In space, everything and everyone in the shuttle is weightless. So if an astronaut drops a pen, it doesn't fall to the ground. It simply floats in the air.

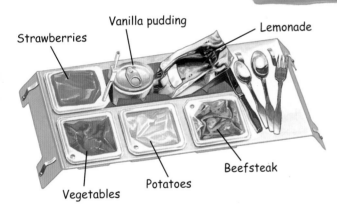

Strawberries

Vanilla pudding

Lemonade

Beefsteak

Potatoes

Vegetables

▶ Sleeping bags are stuck to the cabin walls so that they don't float around. The astronauts wear a mask to block out the light. They are woken by music, beamed up from Earth.

▲ Shuttle astronauts have around 100 different types of food to choose from. Some food is dried and has to be mixed with water. Drinks are sucked through tubes so drops of liquid don't float around the cabin.

Space shuttle toilet

◀ Astronauts have to clip themselves to the seat when they use the toilet, or they might float away.

The shuttle carries up to seven people. The commander, in the left seat, is in charge of the spacecraft. The pilot helps the commander.

Mission specialists are trained to do a particular job on the mission such as launching a satellite.

The commander, pilot, and mission specialists are all astronauts. Extra crew members, called payload specialists, are not. They may be scientists or doctors who do experiments in the Spacelab, or engineers who operate special equipment.

23

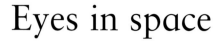

Eyes in space

Navigational satellite

A satellite floats silently in space, its camera pointing at the swirling clouds of a violent hurricane far below. Weather satellites watch Earth and its weather all day and night. Other satellites beam telephone calls and television programs all over the world. There are hundreds of satellites orbiting Earth. They have become so important that it is difficult to imagine our world without them.

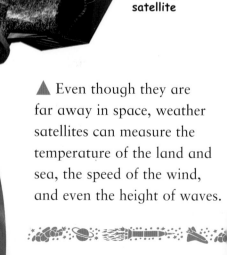

Weather satellite

▲ Even though they are far away in space, weather satellites can measure the temperature of the land and sea, the speed of the wind, and even the height of waves.

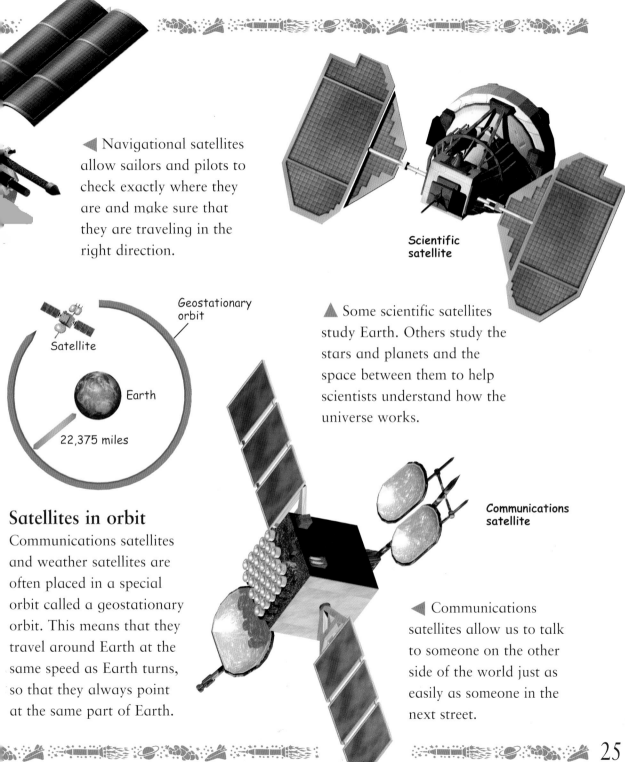

◀ Navigational satellites allow sailors and pilots to check exactly where they are and make sure that they are traveling in the right direction.

Scientific satellite

Geostationary orbit

Satellite

Earth

22,375 miles

▲ Some scientific satellites study Earth. Others study the stars and planets and the space between them to help scientists understand how the universe works.

Satellites in orbit

Communications satellites and weather satellites are often placed in a special orbit called a geostationary orbit. This means that they travel around Earth at the same speed as Earth turns, so that they always point at the same part of Earth.

Communications satellite

◀ Communications satellites allow us to talk to someone on the other side of the world just as easily as someone in the next street.

The Hubble Telescope

Stars look so beautiful because they twinkle like diamonds, but twinkling makes it difficult for astronomers to see them clearly through a telescope. Twinkling is caused by swirling streams of warm and cold air around Earth bending the starlight in different ways.

A telescope in space has the best view of the stars because there is no air in space to make them twinkle. The biggest telescope in space is the Hubble Space Telescope, which was launched from a space shuttle in 1990.

Repairing the Hubble

When the Hubble was launched, astronomers discovered that its view was blurred because it had a faulty mirror. Shuttle astronauts mended the telescope in 1993. Since then, the Hubble has been sending clear pictures back to Earth.

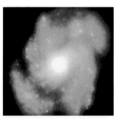

Before repair

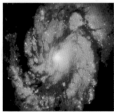

After repair

▶ The Hubble has two large, flat solar panels—one on each side. They make electricity from sunlight in order to power the Hubble's instruments. It sends its pictures to Earth by radio.

Space probes

Every 175 years, the giant planets Jupiter, Saturn, Uranus, and Neptune line up. This means that a spacecraft can visit all of them in one trip. Two space probes, Voyagers 1 and 2, traveled all the way to these planets. They sent back some of the most beautiful pictures we have ever seen—of stormy orange and white clouds over Jupiter, volcanoes erupting on Jupiter's moons, and the broad, flat rings around Saturn.

Journey to the stars

Tiny space probes have visited all eight planets in the solar system. A few have even left the solar system altogether. Pioneer 10, launched in 1972, is the farthest away. The last, very weak signal was received from it in 2003, when it was more than six billion miles from Earth. A final attempt to contact the probe in 2006 received no response.

Mariner

Mariner 9 orbited Mars in 1971, and Mariner 10 visited Venus and Mercury in 1974.

▲ The Voyager probes carry discs with pictures and sounds from Earth in case they are found by beings from another world.

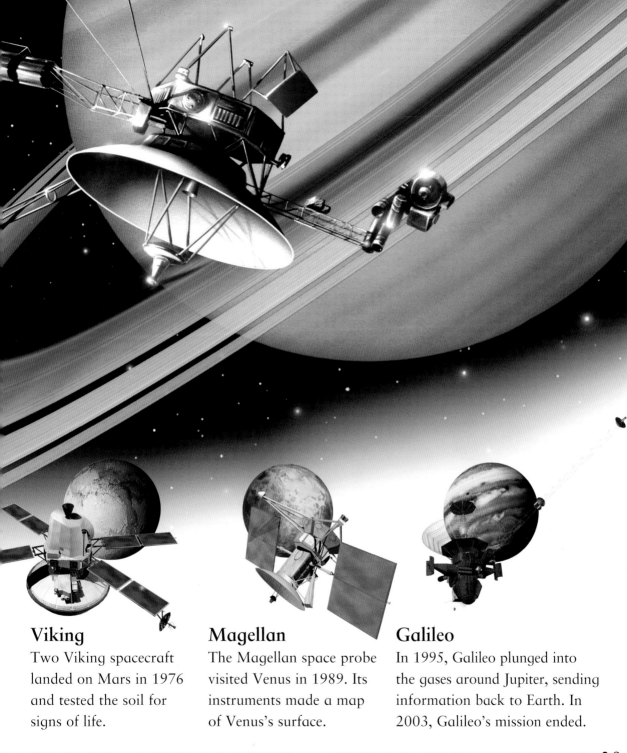

Viking
Two Viking spacecraft landed on Mars in 1976 and tested the soil for signs of life.

Magellan
The Magellan space probe visited Venus in 1989. Its instruments made a map of Venus's surface.

Galileo
In 1995, Galileo plunged into the gases around Jupiter, sending information back to Earth. In 2003, Galileo's mission ended.

Space stations

In the future, astronauts will visit the planets. Perhaps people will even live on Mars. But before this can happen, engineers need to learn how to build spacecraft for flights lasting years instead of days or weeks, and scientists need to study how very long space flights affect astronauts. The first step is to build a large space station in orbit around Earth.

Space Station Freedom

In 1984, plans were announced for a permanently manned, Earth-orbiting, international space station. However, after cutbacks, the project became part of the International Space Station in 1993.

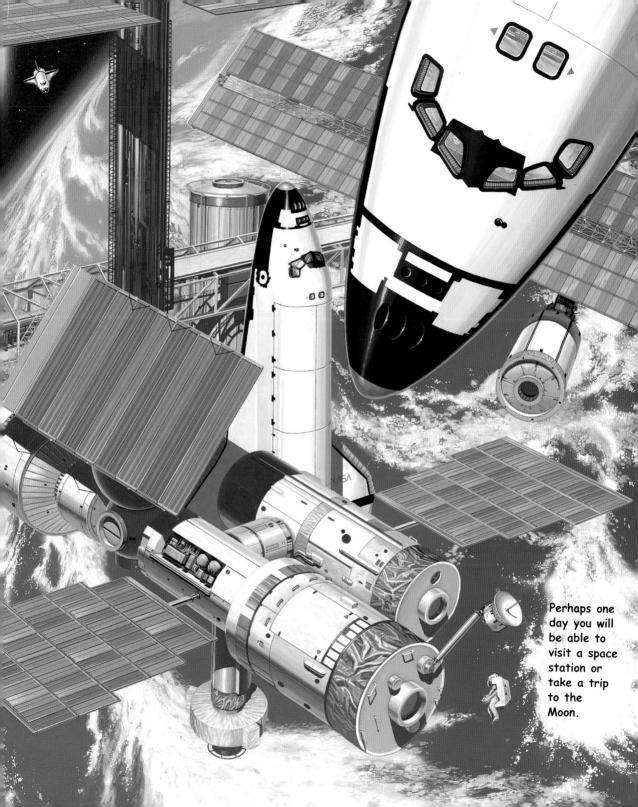

Perhaps one
day you will
be able to
visit a space
station or
take a trip
to the
Moon.

Glossary

astronaut A space traveler.

atmosphere The layer of gases that surround a planet or moon. Earth's atmosphere, or air, is made mainly of three gases—nitrogen, oxygen, and carbon dioxide.

booster An extra rocket used to help launch a larger rocket or the space shuttle.

capsule A small spacecraft with just enough room inside to fit in the crew.

countdown The preparations for the launch of a rocket as a clock ticks backward to zero—the moment when the rocket fires and takes off.

EVA Extra Vehicular Activity—another name for a spacewalk.

gravity The force that pulls everything down to the ground and keeps the planets in orbit around the Sun and satellites in orbit around planets.

launch pad The platform that a rocket or space shuttle stands on for takeoff.

moon A small world that orbits a planet. Every planet except for Mercury and Venus has at least one moon. A moon is a natural satellite.

Moon Buggy An electric car used by some of the Apollo astronauts to drive around on the Moon.

NASA National Aeronautics and Space Administration—the organization that runs American space flights.

orbit The path of a satellite around a planet or a planet around the Sun.

payload Cargo carried by a rocket or space shuttle.

planet A world in orbit around the Sun.

reentry Coming back into, or reentering, Earth's atmosphere from space.

satellite An object in orbit around a planet. A moon is a natural satellite. A spacecraft is an artificial satellite.

solar system The Sun and everything that orbits it, including the planets, their moons, asteroids, and comets.

space probe An unmanned spacecraft sent far away from Earth to find out more about the Sun, the planets, or their moons.

spaceship Any spacecraft that carries people.

space station A large, manned spacecraft that is kept in space for several years.

space suit The special clothes worn by astronauts to protect them when they go outside their spacecraft.

splashdown Landing a spacecraft in the sea.

thruster A tiny rocket engine fired to nudge a spacecraft into a new position.